Chakra Balancing

**COPYRIGHT © 20202 TH PUBLISHING COMPANY
ALL RIGHTS RESERVED.
WRITTEN BY MRS TOMEKA ARTHUR**

Joy & Happiness
is Good for the Soul

Wisdom & Knowledge
is Good for the Mind

Be led by the spirit in doing good, giving back
and loving others.
Be mindful that you have supreme
power over worldly things.
As the mind wanders, bring peace through affirmations,
It allows positive energy to flow to and from you.
Be mindful to care; for all emotions and actions
will be reflected through your body

SPIRIT OF POWER

Affirmations

Wisdom imparted from the knowledge of your inner self brings peace and love

POWER OF LOCATION

Energy Setting

Plants, colorful images, inspiring quotes, comfortable sitting furniture, soft rugs and pillows, music, and candles

BODY

Love

Positive energy is formed from self care and all knowing in the power of self

EXERCISE

Yoga

Reiki and kundalini energy allows organs to align and balance chakras

SOUND MIND

Meditation

Positive thinking allows the highest vibration of joy

CREATE YOUR HAPPY SPACE

Have a positive energy

Practice mindfulness and meditation

Be in the company of good people

Bring light and color to balance vibration

Add value to your family and community

Claim your affirmations daily

Spread love and affection

Relaxation and declutter the mind

Encourage every living thing

Focus on positive relationships starting with self love

Exercise and Yoga

Eat healthy and detox

Identify your physical and emotional needs

Essential Oil Blends
Oils and Butters for wellness and beauty

The most beneficial moisturizers are made from cocoa butter, shea butter, and mango butter

Use these combinations of essential oils with carrier oils; jojoba, sweet almond, avocado, and coconut

Anxiety - Holy basil, Helichrysum & Roman chamomile

Increase happiness and Raise vibration - ylang ylang, lavender, orange, frankincense, rose, and vetiver

Relaxation - lavender, bergamot, Roman chamomile, frankincense, rose, and ylang ylang

Reduce pain - peppermint, lavender, eucalyptus, rosemary, and turmeric

OILS TO KEEP REGULARLY
Lavender
Peppermint
Orange
Eucalyptus
Tea tree
Lemongrass

ROOT

LOM
AFFIRMATIONS

I am Grounded, I am Secure, I am Safe, I am Connected to Nature

I am connected to the Earth having a survival instinct, confidence, foundation of balance, enthusiasm, strength, stamina, focus, discipline, staying healthy, and being beware of my limits

LOCATION base of spine

- IN BALANCE brings cheerfulness, fearless, courage and good health

- OUT OF BALANCE lower abdomen is affected, constipation, diarrhea, hemorrhoids, kidney problems, sciatica, and back problems

- ORGANS connected lungs, skin, kidneys, large intestine, and rectum

- FOODS to help balance the root chakra are proteins and vegetables (red)

- YOGA POSES Warrior I, Eagle Pose, Tree Pose, Child's Pose

CRYSTALS garnet, ruby, red tiger eye, and red jasper

ESSENTIAL OILS vetiver, patchouli, sandalwood, ginger, cypress, frankincense, and cedarwood

R O O T

Root Chakra Clearing

Right hand over left between your legs

Beams of light coming out of your feet and entering the earth to no end
Feeling connected to the trees an soil connecting to the roots of the earth

Breathe in I am Grounded
Breathe out weakness

Breathe in I am connected to the earth
Breathe out shakiness

Breathe in I am grounded

Breathe in my root chakra is open
Breathe out my root chakra is closed

Sacral

VOM
AFFIRMATIONS
I feel desirable, I embrace my sexuality

Connected to Earth and Water bring in energy, let go of shame, embrace passion, reproductive nature, sensuality nurture healthy relationships

LOCATION lower pelvic area

- IN BALANCE brings sensation, pleasure, focus, relation to self change and how to deal with it, healthy lower abdomen, outgoing, sense of humor, comfortable with sexuality, positive, enjoy life, develop, grow, and ability to work with others creatively

- OUT OF BALANCE guilt, anxiety, unpredictability, clinginess

- ORGANS connected lower abdomen urinary circulatory and reproductive systems

- FOODS to help balance the sacral chakra are sweet fruits and nuts

- YOGA POSES Goddess, Dancers Pose, and Pigeons Pose

CRYSTALS citrine

ESSENTIAL OILS patchouli, amber, citrus, sandalwood, jasmine, ylang ylang, and clary sage

Sacral

Sacral Chakra Clearing

Right hand over left in front of navel

Breathe in I am worthy
Breathe out congestion

Breathe in it is safe to express my emotions
Breathe out fear of speaking

Breathe in my sacral chakra is open

Breathe out my sacral chakra is closed

Solar Plexus

ROM
AFFIRMATIONS

I will act with courage, I honor myself, My potential is unlimited Connected to Fire through personal power, high self esteem, trusting your direction, growing, achieving what you want, have clear thinking, having inner strength, will to bring together and not divide, self acceptance, and social responsibility

LOCATION stomach above navel

- IN BALANCE will develop a healthy will, independence in action and thought knowing your personal power, power in unification and a great deal of energy

- OUT OF BALANCE low self esteem, swayed by others opinions, jealousy, anger, frustration, doubts, confusion, ulcers, upset stomach,

- ORGANS connected are digestive system, liver, stomach, gall bladder, pancreas, spleen

- FOODS to help balance starches, seeds and dairy

- YOGA POSES Sun Salutations, Boat Pose, and Mountain Pose

CRYSTALS citrine, tigers eye, golden topaz, and moonstone

ESSENTIAL OILS geranium, juniper, marjoram, lemon, cinnamon, and fennel

Solar Plexus

Solar Plexus Chakra Clearing
Right hand over left in front over ribs

Breathe in I am Strong
Breathe out I am weak

Breathe in I am confident
Breathe out low self esteem

Breathe in I can do anything
Breathe out I am Afraid to try

Breathe in I am confident
Breathe out I am not enough

Breathe in my Solar Plexus Chakra is open
Breathe out my Solar Plexus Chakra is closed

Heart

YOM
AFFIRMATIONS

I love myself and others, I am an Expression of Love,
I am Worthy of Love, I forgive myself and others

Connected to Air through love, compassion, joy, trust, receive and give respect, and ultimate healing

LOCATION Heart region

- IN BALANCE enhances state of being, higher goals, social awareness, openness, devotion, joy, peace, forgiveness, acceptance, kindness, without an ego, unconditional love, and being fearless

- OUT OF BALANCE causes heart condition, high blood pressure, respiratory issues, arthritis of the arms, lack of sensitivity, arrogance, selflessness, sadness, and depression

- ORGANS connected are circulatory and respiratory systems, breast, chest and shoulders

- FOODS to help balance are leafy vegetables

- YOGA POSES Camel Pose, Cobra Pose, Upward-facing Dog Pose

CRYSTALS quartz, emerald, malachite, and aventurine

ESSENTIAL OILS bergamot, rose, pine, geranium, cypress and ylang ylang

Heart

Heart Chakra Clearing

Right hand over left mid chest

Breathe in I am lovable
Breathe out I am not lovable

Breathe in it is safe to love others
Breathe out it is not safe to love

Breathe in my heart chakra is open
Breathe out my heart chakra is closed

Breathe in I am not affected by past hurt
Breathe out past pain

Breathe in I am free from past pain from past love
Breathe out past pain of past love

Breathe in I am Love
Breathe out grief hate jealousy envy lust

Throat

HOM
AFFIRMATIONS

I speak Truth, I am Honest

Connected to Ether through truth, honesty, effectiveness, clear communication of feelings and ideas, self expression involved with verbal expression of thoughts and feelings of lower chakras, connects our feelings and intuition with our thoughts form our future through verbal expression

LOCATION Base of Throat

- IN BALANCE helps to share ideas and information, throat is physically healthy, creativity, inspiration, honesty and compassion

- OUT OF BALANCE causes sore throats, loss of voice, neck or throat conditions over under active thyroid, headache from neck muscle, tension, insomnia, flu, and judgment

- ORGANS connected neck, voice box, airway in the throat, thyroid, and metabolism of the entire body

- FOODS to help balance are fruits, juice, herbs, tea and water

- YOGA POSES supported Shoulder Stand, Circling The Neck, Supported Headstand, and Fish Pose

CRYSTALS sodalite, turquoise, and aquamarine

ESSENTIAL OILS sandalwood, eucalyptus, bergamot, tea tree, and chamomile

Throat

Throat Chakra Clearing

Right hand over left over throat

Breathe in I speak truth
Breathe out afraid to speak my truth

Breathe in it is safe to speak my truth
Breathe out desire to be mean, sarcastic

Breathe in I speak my truth to others
Breathe out congestion

Breathe in my throat chakra is open
Breathe out my throat chakra is closed

Third Eye

OM
AFFIRMATIONS

I see Clearly, I Trust My Decisions, I am Aware Connected to Light through inner vision, spiritual guidance, wisdom, insight, pure essence, intuition, imagination visualization and clairvoyance

LOCATION brow level

- IN BALANCE helps to work with your creativity and beliefs, your intellect, listening to your intuition, observe thoughts and feelings without over attachment, fulfillment of ideas and direction

- OUT OF BALANCE brings headaches, earache, sinus ache, insomnia, anxiety, depression, and lack of concentration

- ORGANS connected are the brain and nervous system, ear, nose, eyes, sinus, hormonal system, and pituitary gland in the brain

- FOODS to help balance are purple kale, grapes, blueberries, broccoli, and plums

- YOGA POSES Easy Pose, Childs Pose, and Cat/Cow Pose

CRYSTALS lapis lazuli, blue sapphire, sodalite, agate, labradorite

ESSENTIAL OILS jasmine, rosemary, lavender, peppermint, and cedarwood

Third Eye Chakra Clearing

Right hand over left hand over eye brows

Breathe in clarity
Breathe out confusion

Breathe in my third eye chakra is open
Breathe out my third eye chakra is closed

Crown

SILENCE
AFFIRMATIONS

I am Divine, I am Spiritual Being, I am One with Infinite Source, I am at Peace Connected to pure light and source of creation through spirituality, boundlessness, divinity, being conscious, connection to higher self, eliminate ego, and rejuvenation

LOCATION top of head

- IN BALANCE help to transcend materialism and let go of physical attachment; highest state of consciousness, spiritual enlightenment, self realization and sense of unity with others, knowledge of wisdom and enlightenment

- OUT OF BALANCE causes cerebral tumors, increased head pressure, depression, insomnia, low energy, fatigue, psychoses, and neuroses

- ORGANS connected are the brain, whole nervous system, and pineal gland

- FOOD fasting

- YOGA Headstand

CRYSTALS amethyst and clear quartz

ESSENTIAL OILS myrrh, neroli, sandalwood, frankincense, and lavender

Crown Chakra Clearing

Right hand over left over crown of head

Breathe in I am Connected to the sun
Breathe out disconnected

Breathe in I am energy
Breathe out congestion

Breathe in I am universal energy
Breathe out spinning

Breathe in my crown chakra is open
Breathe out my crown chakra is closed

TOMEKA ARTHUR   JANUARY 2, 2021

Spirit, Mind & Body

Meditation - Thought Processing, Relaxation & Mental Well-Being

Meditation is not the process of stopping Thought; it is acknowledging one Thought at a time to understand the moment and process resolution.

Breathing, exercising and relaxation are essential to successful meditation practice. Finding an accurate breathing technique that works for your body, stretching to loosen muscle tightening to release tension, creating an upright (aligned back, neck & head) sitting position (pose) for relaxation and a locating a quiet place (one without distractions) to enter into your meditative stanza. Know your purpose, your goal and focus; allowing your mental clarity to overtake body movement and sound.

1

BREATHING
Inhaling & Exhaling

Natural inhalation of breaths allows body cells to receive the energy it needs to perform digestion, growth, healing and detoxing.

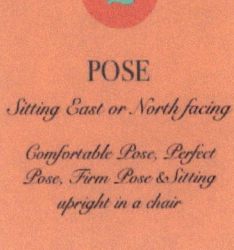

2

POSE
Sitting East or North facing

Comfortable Pose, Perfect Pose, Firm Pose & Sitting upright in a chair

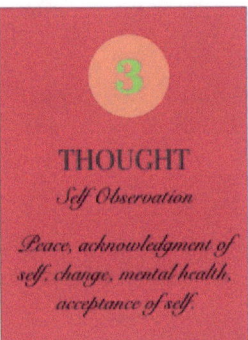

3

THOUGHT
Self Observation

Peace, acknowledgment of self, change, mental health, acceptance of self.

Chakra Balancing Overall Well Being

Aromatherapy aids in mental and physical wellbeing

Crystal Vibrations brings Healing & Protection

TOMEKA ARTHUR   DECEMBER 18, 2020

Spirit, Mind & Body

Essential Oils ~ Aromatherapy, Natural Cleanser & Holistic Healing

Essential oils are highly used in aromatherapy and natural remedies. Essential derives from the word quintessential {the embodying or possessing the essence of something}

Essential oils are natural inhibitors deriving from nature botanicals. The organic essential oils are used in prescription medicine, household cleaners and beauty care products. Holistically quintessential oils are highly recognized for self healing, raising your vibration {inner being, mentally and physically}, the embodiment of the spirit, mind and body, air purifier and meditative aiding.

1

FIXED OILS
Non-volatile

They don't evaporate into the air

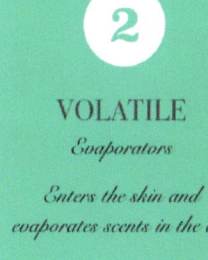

2

VOLATILE
Evaporators

Enters the skin and evaporates scents in the air

3

EXTRACTION
From Plants

Flowers, leaves, roots, barks and peels

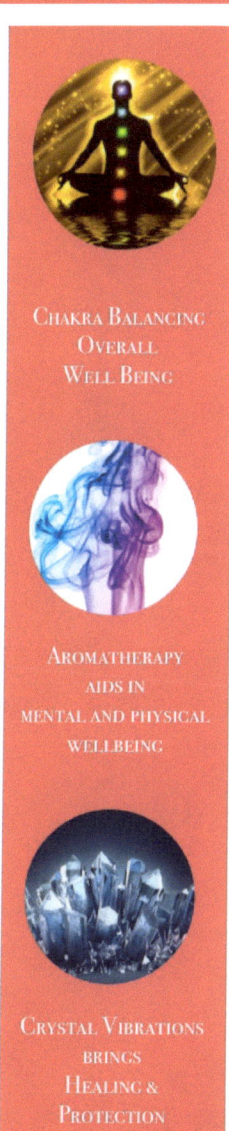

Chakra Balancing Overall Well Being

Aromatherapy aids in mental and physical wellbeing

Crystal Vibrations brings Healing & Protection

7 TIPS FOR POSITIVE THINKING
THOUGHTS ARE THE GATEWAY TO RAISING YOUR VIBRATION

- Do Not Accept Negative Thinking
  - Changing the thought immediately

- Always Make Sure You Are Happy
  - Happiness Allows Positive Vibration To Reciprocate

- Do Not Allow Others Negative Speech In
  - Removing Ourselves From Negative Conversation

- Not Speaking Negatively
  - Continuously Working on Changing Our Speech

- Not Repeating The Thought Mentally
  - Do Not Continue To Think About Anything That Doesn't Result In Happiness, Positivity, and Wholeness

- Not Repeating Negative Actions
  - No Resistance To Positive Energy And Happy Thoughts Will Allow Alignment With Law Of Attraction

- Affirmations
  - Speaking Positive Assurance In Strength and Knowing

7 WAYS TO PLAN AHEAD TO STAY FOCUSED

HOW TO BECOME SUPER PRODUCTIVE

- ORGANIZATION

- PRIORITIZE
    - Complete the tasks with the earliest deadlines and that are most important

- MAKE A SCHEDULE
    - Always prepare for the next day it cuts out the time ordering your tasks

- WRITE DOWN YOUR GOALS AND DAILY TO DO LIST
    - Update this list as necessary to move forward and stay on task

- KNOW WHAT YOU NEED TO MEET YOUR GOALS
    - Be proud, excited and happy about meeting your goals

- BE CONFIDENT
    - Don't allow any denial to keep you from moving forward

- MAKE A DAILY LIMIT TO NOT OVER EXHAUST YOURSELF
    - Take time to meditate, exercise and eat healthy

Chakra Balancing Overall Well Being

The flow of energy balances overall well-being

Aromatherapy aids in mental and physical wellbeing

Crystal Vibrations brings Healing & Protection

Color healing Visualization brings happiness

Books

"Our Beloved Angel:
Legend Gejaune Tahsheem King Arthur
"Our Beloved Nana:
Eldora Fig Dalrymple"
"Faith & Inspiration:
Book of Prayers & Affirmations
"B.Q.E. 2 Da L.I.E: Brooklyn's Big Zill Meets
Lil Meek From Wyandanch"

Certifications

Chakra Healing
Reiki Master or Teacher Course
Mindfulness Practice
The Complete Meditation Course
Complete Guide To Essential Oils and Aromatherapy
Introduction To Crystal Healing
Color Therapy For Kundalini And
Chakra Healing

www.ingramcontent.com/pod-product-compliance
Lightning Source LLC
Chambersburg PA
CBHW042129040426

42450CB00002B/129